# BEAUTIFUL RAGWORK

# BEAUTIFUL RAGWORK

## LIZZIE REAKES

Over 20 hand-hooked designs for floors, walls, furniture, and accessories

St. Martin's Press  New York

For my daughter and little friend Heidi and to Master Werewolfs

Conceived and produced by Breslich & Foss Ltd., London

Printed and bound in Hong Kong

www.stmartins.com

ISBN 0-312-30395-5

Text by Lizzie Reakes
Photography by Shona Wood
Designed by Janet James
Commissioned by Janet Ravenscroft
Project managed by Katy Lord

Library of Congress Cataloging-in-Publication Data available

First U.S. Edition: December 2002

10 9 8 7 6 5 4 3 2 1

# contents

# Introduction

Fleece or fabric was traditionally hooked through a backing cloth to form a thick material for protection against extreme weather conditions. Worn on the body, hung on walls, or lain on floors, the basic technique was developed by many generations through different cultures worldwide: the ancient Egyptians created a form of raised embroidery that left a looped surface, and early settlers in Scandinavia hooked wool through a backing cloth and wore it to keep out the cold.

Contemporary ragwork has its roots in traditional North American rag-rug making: an age-old craft that epitomized the "make do and mend" ethic. Rugs were usually made on a frame, and rug-making tools were fashioned from masonry nails, bent and filed into hook shapes, or wooden clothes pegs sharpened into points. Unwanted fabrics were cut up and hooked through a backing cloth made from burlap (sacking). Fabric was cut into either long strips or short clippings and hooked or poked through the burlap. Gradually patterns emerged and became more sophisticated, taking inspiration from the landscape, animals, and flowers as well as simple

geometric designs. In time, commemorative text began to appear on the rugs: was this the origin of the "welcome" doormat?

Today ragwork is not just associated with rugs. It is used together with stitching and appliqué to make accessories for fashion and interiors. Ragwork is an exciting contemporary textile craft, exhibited internationally in art and craft shows. Ragwork designs can be found hanging alongside quilts, and sharing gallery space with ceramics, glassware, paintings, and jewelry. The appeal of ragwork is huge, largely because it is an economical, environmentally friendly, and creatively inspiring way to recycle old clothes.

In *Beautiful Ragwork*, textile artist Lizzie Reakes shows you how fabrics can be recycled and rejuvenated into beautiful artifacts for the home, or as unique, stylish gifts for family and friends. She gives inspiring examples of how to combine different colors and textures to achieve wonderful results. There are step-by-step projects to create rugs, wall hangings, and fashion accessories. Above all, *Beautiful Ragwork* shows you how different fabrics can be used together to create stunning effects.

# materials

The picture opposite shows the most important materials and some of the decorative elements used in this book.
These include backing fabrics, such as burlap and felt, and decorative accents like the ballerina figurine.
Recycling lies at the heart of ragwork: the fabric from all sorts of old clothes can be reused in ragwork projects.
Old buttons or beads can be used to add texture, and ring pulls from drinks cans sewn to the back of small
wall hangings make excellent hoops from which to hang them.

black Velcro strip
red Velcro strip
blue Velcro strip
brown parcel paper

rug canvas
burlap
green felt
white nylon net

plain white paper
blue and purple pom-poms
pink roses on wires
assorted beads

green mirror motifs
ring pull from drinks can
wooden toggle
plaited red wool

wide blue ribbon
green ribbon
yellow ribbon
tartan ribbon

yellow wool
navy and white microdot and
  striped printed cotton jersey
red satin
pink embroidered sari fabric
red nylon net

plastic ballerina figure
assorted buttons
hair grips
squeaker
metal hairband

strips of fabric:
mauve cotton jersey
red polyester
yellow cotton jersey
red felt

mauve tapestry wool
polyester toy stuffing
blue tapestry wool

black sewing thread
linen thread
red sewing thread
white sewing thread

blue pom-pom edged braiding
box of embroidery threads

red silk roses

# equipment

The equipment used to make the projects in this book is shown opposite. Specialist tools may, if necessary, be substituted by those more easily available, for example a crochet hook may be used instead of a ragwork hook. However, using the correct equipment will make the projects easier to complete. Similarly, the larger projects can be hooked without the use of a frame, but it is easier to hook through burlap on a large scale when it is held taut. The large wooden peg frame in the picture can be adapted to different sized projects by moving the pegs.

large wooden peg frame,
    60 x 60 in. (150 x 150 cm)

bottle of latex

colored pencils

big eye tapestry needle
medium embroidery needle
sewing needle
crochet hook, size 3.5

red and blue plastic
    embroidery hoops, 6³/₄ in.
    (17 cm) in diameter
dressmaking scissors
wooden embroidery hoop,
    10 in. (25 cm) in diameter
wooden embroidery hoop,
    12³/₄ in. (32 cm) in diameter

ruler
tape measure
thin felt pen
thick felt pen

small scissors
artist's stretching frame,
    15³/₄ x 15³/₄ in. (40 x 40 cm)
staples

pencil
staple gun

hook

box of dressmaking pins

# types of fabric

Ten different types of fabric are shown here as plain fabric swatches together with hooked cut- and loop-pile surfaces. As you will see, some fabrics are more successful than others when hooked, and some material can look surprisingly different when hooked in either a cut- or loop-pile surface. The fabrics shown represent only a selection of those available to use for hooking. If you aren't sure about the end result of using a certain type of fabric, test it out first on a small piece of burlap. Hook a loop-pile surface then trim the tops off some of the loops to see what a cut-pile surface will look like.

## Red tartan

This fabric is not suitable for hooking in large areas as both the cut-pile (left) and loop-pile (right) surfaces can fray. Tartan is not a durable fabric when hooked, so is not good for use in rugs. It is best used in small areas for wall pieces or fashion accessories in a loop-pile surface to add color and texture to complement wool, felt, or cotton jersey.

## Red silk

This fabric's color is much darker when the pile is cut. The light bounces off a loop pile (right), making the fabric seem paler. Silk is most suitable for fashion accessories or for wall pieces as it tends to fray slightly. For rugs, use silk in small areas surrounded by tougher more hard-wearing wool or cotton jersey.

## Printed cotton jersey

Printed cotton completely changes its identity when hooked. The loop pile (left) demonstrates how both the front and back of the fabric will appear when hooked (by turning the fabric on your hook it is possible to control the loops so that only the printed side shows, but this is very laborious). The cut-pile surface (right) is more successful as an overall pattern—it is quite impressionistic, therefore good for adding a painterly feel to large backgrounds. Cotton jersey is hard-wearing and suitable for all projects.

## Rusty red polyester/elastane mix

This stretchy fabric is a joy to hook as it does not fray, is hard-wearing, and can be incorporated into any project. Polyester/elastane mix looks great when the cut-pile surface (right) and low (or high) loop-pile surface (left) are combined as the loop reflects the light and the cut surface brings out a darker, squiggly texture. Choose old lycra-mix sportswear or swimming costumes for similar results.

## Pink felt

Felt is very good for backgrounds on rugs or where there are large areas of one color. When the pile of felt is cut (left) it creates a cozy, soft texture. When felt is looped (right) it has a very neat surface. The color of the felt doesn't vary much whether a cut- or loop-pile surface is created. Felt works well for all projects, especially when introduced with appliqué.

## Pink and orange printed silk

When the pile is cut (bottom) the pattern on the silk becomes muddy in color. It works better as a low loop-pile surface (top) as the colors are lighter and brighter. Good for fashion and wall projects, plain and printed silk can be used in small areas for floors if left as a low loop-pile surface.

## Orange and mustard open weave rayon/linen mix

Loose or open weave fabrics are not very good for hooking as once they are cut into strips the fabric frays. This fabric is not successful when the loop surface is cut (left) as it can shed. As a low loop pile (right), it can be used in moderation.

## Plum wool

Wool works beautifully hooked either as a cut-surface pile (right) or loop-surface pile (left), and is a great fabric for filling in backgrounds or large areas of flat color. Source old woolens, boil wash them in the machine and they cut up with minimum fraying and almost a felt-like appearance.

## Fuchsia cotton jersey

Cotton jersey is extremely versatile—it looks and feels great when hooked in a short or long loop (top) as well as when cut (right). It does not fray and is the best fabric to use for a long loop with spaced intervals. This is the best fabric for children or beginners to use as it virtually hooks itself!

## Red nylon net

Nylon net is available in many colors. It can be cut into strips as wide as 1¾ in. (4 cm) and folded or twisted over the end of the hook. Combining two layers of different colored net creates a color blend of a painterly quality when cut. This can be used to great effect for a landscape or still life image. Because of its abrasive texture when hooked in either a loop-pile surface (right) or a cut-pile surface (left), nylon net makes an excellent front door mat.

# techniques

## hooking: low loop-pile surface

**1** Place the burlap in the embroidery hoop. Push the hook through the burlap from front to back. Take a strip of fabric and loop the end of the strip onto the hook at the back of the burlap. Pull the hook with the fabric hooked onto it through to the front.

**2** Working one or two burlap threads away from the first "hole," push the hook through to the back of the burlap. Fold the fabric strip over the end of the hook with a pinch-like grip.

**3** Pull the hook back through the burlap, bringing the fabric with it, to make a loop approximately ¼ in. (5 mm) high. Continue in this way until the project is complete. The ends of fabric strips should be hooked through to the front then trimmed so they are slightly shorter than the loops when hooking is complete.

# hooking:
# cut-pile surface

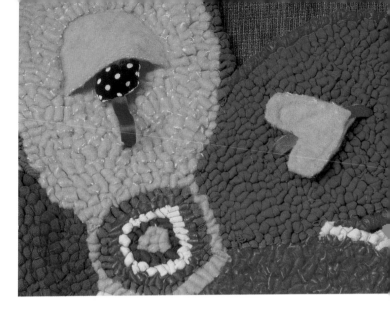

**1** Place the burlap in the embroidery hoop. Follow the method for low loop-pile surface on page 18, but make the loops approximately ³⁄₄ in. (2 cm) high.

# backstitch

Backstitch is a strong stitch and can be used for securing layers of fabric. It is especially good for appliquéd areas.

**2** Continue hooking a row of loops, spaced one or two threads apart from one another, and bring the end of the fabric strip up through the burlap. To make a cut-pile surface, hold the scissors horizontally across the loops. Trim off the tops to make a pile height of approximately ¹⁄₄ in. (5 mm).

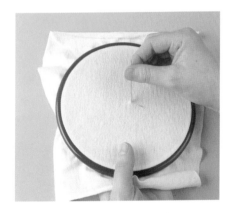

**1** Make a stitch in the fabric ¹⁄₄ in. (5 mm) long then bring the needle through to the front of the fabric ¹⁄₄ in. (5 mm) away from the end of the stitch.

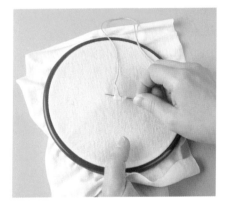

**2** Push the needle through to the back of the fabric as close to the end of the first stitch as possible, bringing it out at the front of the fabric ¹⁄₂ in. (1 cm) away. Continue in this way.

# blanket stitch

Blanket stitch works best when using a thick thread, such as embroidery thread or tapestry wool. For further decoration use a contrasting color, for example appliqué a pink felt heart motif and use a blue thread (or wool) to stitch it in place.

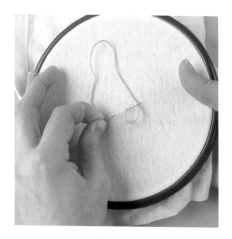

**1** Pull the needle through to the front of the fabric. Make a horizontal stitch ½ in. (1 cm) long that ends ½ in. (1 cm) above the point at which the thread comes through to the front. Ensure that the needle passes over the loose thread.

**2** Gently pull the thread to create the first stitch.

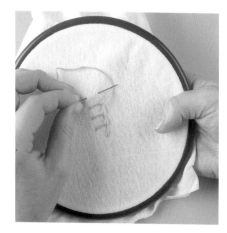

**3** Make another horizontal stitch ½ in. (1 cm) above the first, again ensuring the needle passes over the loose thread, and continue in this way.

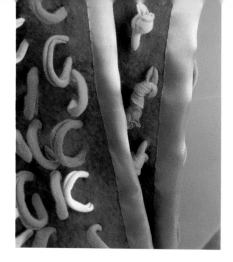

# slipstitch

Slipstitch is great for invisible hemming. It is also the best stitch to use when sewing a burlap or felt cloth to the back of a hooked or appliquéd piece of work.

**1** Use pins to secure the pieces of fabric to be slipstitched together. Push the needle through the top piece of fabric. Catch the fabric underneath with the needle ¼ in. (5 mm) away and push the needle back up through the top piece of fabric. Continue in this way.

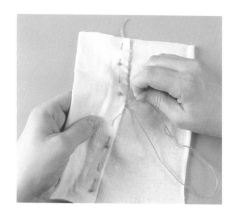

# french knots

French knots add surface texture to appliquéd areas. The size of the knot depends on the thickness of the thread or yarn that you use.

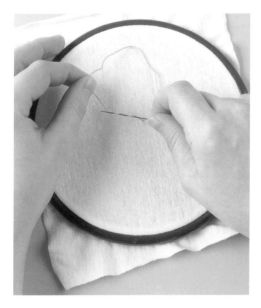

**1**  Push the needle through to the front of the fabric. Place the eye end of the needle against the fabric end of the thread and wind the thread twice around the needle toward the sharp end.

**2**  Push the needle back through the fabric, very close to the first hole.

**3**  Gently pull the thread at the back of the fabric to create the knot.

# crocheted chain

Crocheted chains can be used as decoration either hooked through backing cloth or as hand-sewn detail. By using a wider crochet hook and thicker yarn you can create bigger chain stitches.

**1**  Make a slip loop by tying a knot toward the end of the wool, but feeding the end through the center of the knot before tightening.

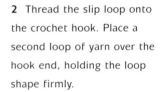

**2**  Thread the slip loop onto the crochet hook. Place a second loop of yarn over the hook end, holding the loop shape firmly.

**3**  Push the first loop over the end of the crochet hook and the loop shape you are holding. Make a third loop over the hook end of the crochet hook, and push the second loop over the end of the hook and the third loop. Continue in this way. To finish, place the end of the wool through the final loop and tie a knot.

# finishing

## using latex

Latex works well as a finishing material as it prevents the burlap from fraying. Latexed pieces can be hand washed, using tepid water and a very mild detergent. Latex is particularly good for finishing curved or shaped pieces, such as hearts or stars. Always use latex in a well-ventilated area and out of reach of children or pets.

**1** Remove the burlap from the frame. Turn the piece face down. Cut around the work leaving a border of approximately ½ in. (1 cm).

**2** Pour some latex into a pot. Use a strip of thick card as a spreader. Dip the card into the latex, then spread a thin layer of latex over the burlap border area.

**3** Wait three to five minutes to allow the latex to dry slightly. It should be still sticky but no longer liquid. Take the scissors and snip from the edge of the burlap border toward the hooking, at intervals of approximately ½ in. (1 cm), around the curved edges.

**4** Fold the burlap over toward the hooked area. Neaten the corners by folding them over to make triangle shapes. Press down firmly.

**5** Push the opposite flaps toward each other and press down.

# attaching a ring pull

Recycle ring pulls from drinks cans as decorative details (below), or by sewing them onto the back of hooked pieces to use as hangers. Linen thread is used as it is extremely strong and cannot be broken by pulling.

**1** On the back of the hooked piece, bring the needle and thread through the burlap and the bottom of the ring pull and tie the end to the length on the needle with a double knot.

**2** Sew over the bottom of the ring pull several times. Push the needle through the burlap and bring it out near the top hole in the ring pull. Sew through this several times to secure the ring pull to the back of the piece.

# backing a square

Square or rectangular projects of any size may be backed in this way. The burlap backing cloth has its edges folded under and placed against the back of the piece, so there is no need to hem it first.

**1**  Cut a piece of burlap large enough to allow a ½ in. (1 cm) border to be turned underneath. Thus, if your hooked square measures 3 x 3 in. (8 x 8 cm) cut a square of burlap 4 x 4 in. (10 x 10 cm). Working at a corner, fold a triangle of burlap in toward the center.

**2**  Fold in the two adjoining sides toward the center so that they meet.

**3**  Pin the folded corner of the burlap to the back of the hooked square, with the rough edges facing inward.

**4**  Fold under the backing burlap at the other three corners in the same way as the first and pin in position.

**5**  Using linen thread, slipstitch all around the square. Remove the pins.

# backing a composite piece

When designing a wall piece or floor rug that has many components making up one large shape, finishing it with Velcro gives you the freedom to change the layout of the piece time and time again. Felt is a good backing cloth as it doesn't fray so doesn't need hemming.

**1** Cut out a felt backing cloth the correct size for the whole piece. Measure half the width of one of the individual hooked squares. In the case of the patchwork rug (page 36) it is 1 1/2 in. (4 cm). Using a thin felt pen mark 1 1/2 in. (4 cm) down from the top of the felt at both sides. With a ruler, draw a horizontal line across the felt joining the marks. Measure down from this marked line; this time the measurement will be the full width of each square, 3 in. (8 cm). Continue marking intervals of 3 in. (8 cm). The final line on the felt should be 1 1/2 in. (4 cm) up from the bottom.

**2** Cut strips of Velcro long enough to be sewn along each marked line. Pull the Velcro strips apart and, working with the female/non-abrasive sides, pin the first strip along the top marked line. Slipstitch around the Velcro strip. Repeat this until each line has a horizontal Velcro strip sewn to it.

**3** Cut each remaining male/abrasive strip into lengths that fit the squares, in this case five lengths of 3 in. (8 cm). Measure a center point on each square. Pin a strip across the center on the back of each square. Using black thread slipstitch the Velcro securely. Repeat this until all of the squares are finished.

**4** Arrange the squares on the felt backing cloth, sticking the Velcro together to hold them in place.

# floors

# floral rug

Give friends and family a warm welcome to your home by placing a cheerful rug in the doorway. Rag rugs are renowned for their durability, so wear and tear is not a problem.

This project was inspired by the psychedelic floral patterns of the 1960s. The lily and surrounding flower shapes have been simplified, and colorful accents added in the shape of scrolls and stars. Rich, jewel-like colors have been chosen in shades of hot reds and vibrant blues.

**Materials**

plain paper
brown paper
burlap, 35½ x 27 in.
  (90 x 68 cm)
fabrics: cotton, nylon, jersey

**Equipment**

pencil
colored pencils
tape measure
thick felt pen
scissors
dressmaking pins
frame, 27½ x 20 in.
  (70 x 50 cm)
staple gun
hook

*Approximate finished size:*
27 x 19 in. (68 x 48 cm)

1 Draw a semicircular shape on plain paper, then fill in the design using colored pencils. On brown paper, measure a semicircular shape 27 in. (68 cm) wide and 19 in. (48 cm) deep at the bottom of the curve. Using the original design for reference, copy the main motifs onto the brown paper template and cut around the outer edge.

**2** Place the brown paper template on the burlap, pin it into position and draw around the shape with the thick felt pen.

**3** Cut out the main motifs from the template and, using the original design for reference, pin them into position on the burlap. Draw around the motif templates with the thick felt pen. Fill in the other details freehand.

**4** Attach the burlap to the frame with the staple gun. Cut the fabrics into strips approximately ¹/₂ in. (1 cm) wide and as long as possible. Begin hooking the central flower using a loop pile.

**5** Continue hooking outward from the central flower, changing color where desired. By using different tones of the same color a painterly effect is created.

**6** Once all areas have been filled, highlight the pattern using a contrasting color. Carefully push the hook back through the burlap, and—leaving the end of the strip underneath—pull up individual loops spaced approximately ³⁄₄ in. (2 cm) apart, and work around the shape leaving spots of color. To finish off, follow the method on page 22.

# latticework rug

This rug is based on a simple latticework pattern. The diamonds of warm reds, yellows, and pinks are framed by diagonal lines of blue, hooked in different shades to make the pattern less rigid. Pom-pom braiding adds a luxurious finishing touch.

**Materials**

plain paper
fabrics: cotton, jersey,
 wool/acrylic in assorted
 colors
2 pieces of burlap,
 33½ x 33½ in.
 (85 x 85 cm) and
 24½ x 24½ in.
 (62 x 62 cm)
linen thread
pom-pom edged braiding,
 3 yards (2.6 m) long
blue thread

**Equipment**

pencil
colored pencils
scissors
thick felt pen
ruler
frame, 31½ x 31½ in.
 (80 x 80 cm)
staple gun
hook
dressmaking pins
needle

*Approximate finished size:*
23½ x 23½ in.
 (60 x 60 cm)

**1** Draw a lattice design on paper and color it in. Select a range of fabrics that match the colors within the design. Prepare the fabrics by cutting them into strips approximately ¾ in. (2 cm) wide and as long as possible.

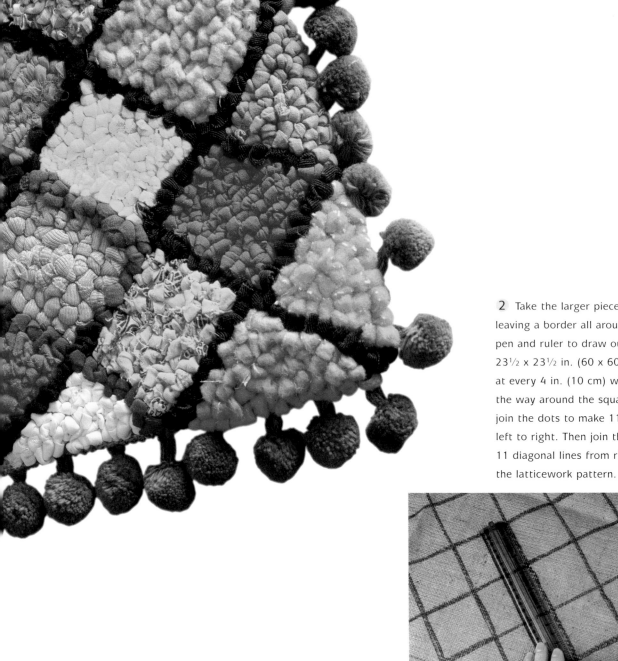

**2** Take the larger piece of burlap, and leaving a border all around, use the thick felt pen and ruler to draw out a square measuring 23½ x 23½ in. (60 x 60 cm). Mark a point at every 4 in. (10 cm) with a dot. Continue all the way around the square. Using the ruler join the dots to make 11 diagonal lines from left to right. Then join the dots to make 11 diagonal lines from right to left, to create the latticework pattern.

**3** Attach the burlap to the frame with the staple gun. Begin hooking the diagonal lines in a dark color, using a loop pile.

**4** Continue hooking the diagonal lines, varying the tones. Fill in the diamond areas with different colors, using the original design for reference.

**5** Once all areas of the pattern are filled, remove the burlap from the frame. To finish off, follow the method on page 22. Then back the piece with the remaining burlap square following the method on page 24. Take the pom-pom edged braiding and pin this to the edge of the rug. Using a double length of blue thread, slipstitch the braiding to the rug (for slipstitch see page 20).

# patchwork rug

This rug is made up of 25 separate squares, each of which is made using a hooked or appliqué technique. The beauty of the piece is that the squares are attached to a backing cloth with Velcro, so they can be moved around to suit your mood.

## HOOKED TECHNIQUE

**Materials**

plain paper
fabrics: wool/acrylic, jersey,
   cotton, nylon
burlap, 8½ x 8½ in.
   (22 x 22 cm)

**Equipment**

pencil
ruler
colored pencils
thick felt pen
embroidery hoop, 6¼ in.
   (16 cm) in diameter
scissors
hook

*Approximate finished size
of each square:*
3 x 3 in. (8 x 8 cm)

*whole rug:*
15¾ x 15¾ in.
   (40 x 40 cm)

**1** Draw a series of squares measuring 3 x 3 in. (8 x 8 cm) on paper. For this project you will need 25 squares in total. Draw a variety of designs within the squares, and use colored pencils to indicate the different colors. Select a range of fabrics to match your color choices.

**2** Draw a square 3 x 3 in. (8 x 8 cm) in the center of the burlap with a thick felt pen. Place the burlap in the embroidery hoop and mark out the chosen design within the square.

**3** Prepare the fabrics by cutting them into strips approximately ¾ in. (2 cm) wide and as long as possible. Begin hooking around the edge of the square in blue.

**4** With yellow wool, fill in the central oval in a slightly taller loop pile than that of the blue edge. With scissors, trim across the top of the yellow loops to create a cut-pile surface.

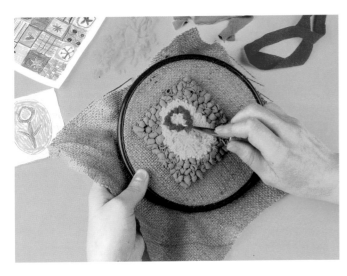

5 Working from the original design, take a red fabric strip and hook the outline flower motif in a loop pile. To finish off, follow the method on page 24.

# APPLIQUÉ TECHNIQUE

## Materials

plain paper
fabrics: felt and cotton
  jersey
embroidery thread
burlap, 8½ x 8½ in.
  (22 x 22 cm)
orange felt heart,
  1¾ x 1¼ in. (4 x 3 cm)
selection of buttons
linen thread

## Equipment

pencil
ruler
colored pencils
scissors
needle
embroidery hoop, 6¼ in.
  (16 cm) in diameter
thick felt pen
hook
dressmaking pins

*Approximate finished size
of each square:*

3 x 3 in. (8 x 8 cm)

*whole rug:*

15¾ x 15¾ in.
  (40 x 40 cm)

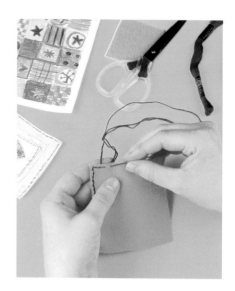

**1** Draw a square measuring 3 x 3 in. (8 x 8 cm) on paper; within this draw a design and color it in. Select a range of fabrics that match the colors within the design. Take the two colors of felt and using the ruler measure two squares, one 3 x 3 in. (8 x 8 cm), the other 2½ x 2½ in. (6 x 6 cm). Cut out both squares.

**2** Take the larger square and using the embroidery thread sew a backstitch border all around (see the method on page 19). Place to one side.

**3** Take the smaller felt square and sew a backstitch around it, as in step 2. Place the burlap in the embroidery hoop. With a ruler and thick felt pen, draw a square measuring 3 x 3 in. (8 x 8 cm). Position the smaller felt square inside this. In the center of the square place the orange heart. Choose a button in a contrasting color, place this in the middle of the heart and stitch it in position through the layers of felt and the burlap with embroidery thread.

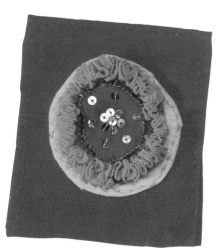

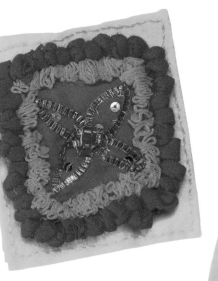

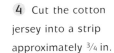

**4** Cut the cotton jersey into a strip approximately ¾ in. (2 cm) wide and as long as possible. Hook around the edge of the square. Remove the burlap from the embroidery hoop and finish it off following the method on page 22.

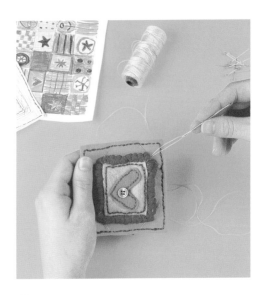

**5** Position and pin the hooked square on top of the larger felt square. Take the linen thread and stitch through both layers to join the squares together.

To join all 25 squares together follow the method on page 25.

# striped floor rug

**striped floor rug** In this rug strips of fabric are hooked through rug canvas rather than burlap. The advantage of this is that a uniform pile and straight stripes are easily achieved due to the regular holes in the rug canvas mesh. This striped rug is made from a variety of discarded material from stretchy T-shirts and lycra sportswear, to thick acrylic blankets.

Create a design keeping in mind the basic striped pattern and your palette of colors. A horizontal stripe of alternating tones can produce stunning effects—rich and dark, hot and warm, or cool and calm—depending on the selection of fabrics. Mix a rainbow of colors for a vibrant look, or choose a variety of shades of a single color. For this rug, multicolored stripes have been combined with a dark blue base.

**Materials**

rug canvas, 40 x 28 in.
  (100 x 71 cm), 3 holes
  per in./25 mm

fabrics: jersey, cotton,
  wool/acrylic, lycra, nylon

**Equipment**

paper
colored pencils
scissors
hook

*Approximate finished size:*
36 x 28 in. (92 x 71 cm)

**1** Sketch a design on paper and color it in. Select a range of fabrics to match the colors of the design.

**2** Cut the fabrics into strips approximately ½ in. (1 cm) wide and as long as possible. Begin hooking the edge. Fold under five rows of canvas so that you are hooking through a double layer for the first five lines.

**3** To change colors, simply push the hook through the previous hole, bring the end of the fabric strip through to the front, and continue hooking along the row in the usual way.

**4** To finish off, make a loop in the last hole, then work back to make a second loop in the previous hole. Bring up the end of the fabric strip and trim it off. The striped rug is ready to use.

## child's activity mat

This bold and bright five-petalled daisy is designed to stimulate a young child's sensory skills. In addition to the texture of the hooked flower shape, each petal features a different element for little hands to explore.

The orange pocket and Velcro for the sun and moon are sewn to the burlap before the background is hooked; the other elements are added afterward. The finished mat is suitable for children over six months old.

### HOOKED FLOWER SHAPE

**Materials**

plain paper
fabric: assorted textures in
    orange, green, blue, red,
    and yellow
burlap, $23\frac{1}{2}$ x $23\frac{1}{2}$ in.
    (60 x 60 cm)
2 orange fabric semicircular
    shapes, 2 x $1\frac{3}{4}$ in.
    (5 x 4 cm)
orange thread
Velcro in blue and red, each
    piece 2 in. (5 cm) long

**Equipment**

pencil
colored pencils
scissors
tape measure
thick felt pen
dressmaking pins
needle
staple gun
frame, $21\frac{1}{2}$ x $21\frac{1}{2}$ in.
    (55 x 55 cm)
hook

*Approximate finished size:*
$19\frac{1}{2}$ in. (50 cm) in diameter

**1** Draw a design on paper and color it in. Select fabrics to match the colors within the design. Prepare the fabrics by cutting them into strips approximately ³/₄ in. (2 cm) wide and as long as possible.

**2** Use a tape measure to find the center of the burlap. With a thick felt pen make a dot, and from this point measure 10 in. (25 cm) outward in five different directions marking all points with a dot. Within this 20 in. (50 cm) diameter area draw out the flower shape. In the center draw five concentric circles, the largest approximately 3 in. (8 cm) in diameter.

**3** Take the blue and red male/ abrasive strips of Velcro and pin them to what will be the blue and red petals (use the original design for reference). With matching threads, sew the Velcro to the burlap.

**4** Take one of the orange semicircular shapes and pin this near the bottom of one of the petals. Sew around it with backstitch (see the method on page 19). Pin the second orange semicircular shape on top of the first. Using matching thread, sew around the curved edge leaving the straight edge open to make a pocket.

**5** Attach the burlap to the frame with a staple gun. Begin hooking the central circle in orange, making a loop-pile surface. Continue working outward with one row of blue and then one row of yellow. Complete hooking around the circle in red, green, and orange—see the original design for reference.

**6** Hook the petal that has the orange pocket on it in orange fabric, then hook an outline in green. Following the original design, continue hooking each petal in the corresponding color. Use a loop pile throughout. Working clockwise around the flower shape, the outline color of each petal will be the same color as the previous petal. When the surface is covered, remove the burlap from the frame. To finish off, follow the method on page 22.

# PADDED SHAPES

### Materials

square of striped fabric,
1¾ x 1¾ in. (4 x 4 cm)
square of microdot fabric,
1¾ x 1¾ in. (4 x 4 cm)
thread in white, blue, and
red
polyester toy stuffing
ribbon in blue and yellow,
each piece 19½ in.
(50 cm) long
circle of silver fabric, 3 in.
(8 cm) in diameter
Velcro in blue and red, each
piece 2 in. (5 cm) long
2 yellow fabric circles, each
2 in. (5 cm) in diameter

### Equipment

dressmaking pins
needle
hook

**7** To make the striped/microdot shape, pin the squares of material together with the patterned surfaces facing inward. Sew a backstitch around the edges, leaving a gap of ½ in. (1 cm). Turn the square inside out, so the patterns are showing, and fill with polyester toy stuffing. Take the length of blue ribbon and place at least ½ in. (1 cm) through the gap. Sew up the gap with the ribbon in place.

Attach this square to the orange petal by hooking the blue ribbon through to the back of the rug. Leave 4 in. (10 cm) of ribbon at the front of the rug so the square can be tucked into the pocket. Tie a knot in the end of the ribbon at the back of the rug and stitch the tied end securely to the rug.

**8** To make the padded moon, take the silver circle and fold it in half so that the wrong side is showing. Pin around the edge. With white thread sew a backstitch around the semicircle, leaving a gap of ½ in. (1 cm). Remove the pins. Turn the semicircle inside out, take a handful of polyester toy stuffing and fill the moon. Sew up the gap. Pin the female/non-abrasive blue Velcro strip on the back and sew it into position with blue thread. Position the moon on the blue petal, over the Velcro strip.

**9** For the sun, take the two yellow circles and yellow ribbon. Cut the yellow ribbon into three equal lengths. Fold the lengths of ribbon so that the ends meet in the middle, leaving loops at either end. Position and pin the three ribbon lengths between the two yellow circles so that each ribbon is lying across the others at the center. Pin around the circles and, using yellow thread, sew around the edge in a backstitch, leaving a gap of ½ in. (1 cm). Take a handful of polyester toy stuffing and fill the sun, then sew up the gap. Pin the female/non-abrasive red Velcro strip on the back and sew it into position with red thread. Place the sun on the Velcro on the red petal.

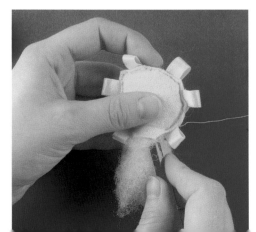

# HEART AND TOGGLE

**10** Take the two orange hearts and pin them together. With orange thread, sew a backstitch around each curved edge and then up to the top, so that there is a channel in the center of the heart. Push the hook up through the center and pull the red ribbon back. Attach the heart to the green petal by hooking the ends of the ribbon through the burlap at the top and at the bottom. Tie the ribbon ends and stitch the tied ends securely to the rug.

**Materials**

2 orange fabric hearts,
 2¼ x 2 in. (6 x 5 cm)
orange thread
red ribbon
green thread
strips of red and green
 fabric
wooden toggle

**Equipment**

dressmaking pins
needle
hook

**11** Take a red strip of fabric approximately 8 in. (20 cm) long and hook it through the yellow petal, leaving a loop of 2¼ in. (6 cm) at the front. Leave the ends at the back of the rug. Take the toggle and a strip of green fabric approximately 12 in. (30 cm) long. Fold the green strip in half, thread the loop end over the toggle, pass the other ends through the loop and pull tight. You may wish to stitch the fabric in place around the toggle with green thread for extra security. Push the hook through to the front of the yellow petal and bring the green fabric ends through to the back of the mat.

**12** Working on the wrong side of the mat, take the red strip ends and the green strip ends and tie them tightly together. Using double thread, stitch the ends securely to the back of the rug.

# windows & walls

## sentimental sampler

Instead of sending birthday greetings with a card, why not create a richly textured sampler? This piece is hand hooked with added appliqué, and makes good use of unwanted buttons. A tiny ballerina is framed by four fabric roses, all done in the birthday girl's favorite colors.

The design shown here is perfect for birthdays, but the basic idea can be adapted to suit all kinds of special events. The birth of a baby, a new house, or a memorable holiday can all be crafted and commemorated in this way, and the background shape altered to suit the occasion. For example, use a heart shape for a wedding sampler or a star for a graduation.

**Materials**

burlap, 13¼ x 13¼ in.
 (34 x 34 cm)
fabrics: cotton, nylon, jersey
gingham, 1½ x 2 in.
 (4 x 5 cm)
plastic figurine
invisible thread
15 buttons
red thread
flower patch
4 fabric roses
red wool

**Equipment**

paper
pencil
colored pencils
scissors
ruler
marker pen
embroidery hoop, 12¼ in.
 (32 cm) in diameter
hook
dressmaking pins
needle

*Approximate finished size:*
8 x 8 in. (20 x 20 cm)

**1** Sketch the design on paper and color it in. Cut the fabric into strips approximately ½ in. (1 cm) wide and as long as possible.

**2** Draw a square 8 x 8 in. (20 x 20 cm) on the burlap and place it in the embroidery hoop. Hook around the outline of the square.

**3** Remove the burlap from the frame, then pin and sew the gingham to the center of the square. Stitch the ballerina figurine in place on the gingham patch with invisible thread.

**4** Place the piece in the embroidery hoop once more. Hook around the gingham patch with a loop pile. For the next five rows, make a cut-pile surface by hooking then cutting across the top of the loops. Continue hooking with a loop pile, changing fabrics as you go, until you reach the edge of the design.

**5** Once all areas are hooked, remove the embroidery hoop and pin the buttons in the shape of a number eight. Sew the buttons in position, then add the flower patch and a rose in each corner of the frame.

**6** Using double-thickness wool, sew a vertical running stitch between the top and bottom rose on the left and right sides of the square. To finish off, follow the method on page 24.

This sampler for a young racing-car enthusiast combines printed cottons and plain fabrics in shades of blue and green. The design is hand hooked with appliquéd patches and raised embroidery details.

# personalized wall tile

Pets are the perfect subject matter for a project piece. Working from a photograph that captures the pet's personality provides all the inspiration needed to create a unique wall tile. Choose fabrics that have a similar color and texture to the animal's coat. Buttons and beads can be used to highlight facial features.

For this personalized wall tile a dog has been chosen. A variety of white fabrics was used for her coat, including some scarf fringing to add texture. The tile combines a cut- and loop-pile surface with appliquéd elements to bring the piece to life: a silver pom-pom tail, a plaited red collar, a football, and a felt heart. She even has a squeaker in her tummy!

## Materials

plain paper
fabrics: wool/acrylic,
    jersey, cotton, nylon, net,
    lycra, felt
burlap, 20 x 20 in.
    (51 x 51 cm)
white cotton fabric,
    2 x 2 in. (5 x 5 cm)
thread in white, red and
    black
squeaker
football patch, 1¼ in.
    (3 cm) in diameter
2 handfuls of polyester toy
    stuffing
3 strands of red knitting
    wool, 8 in. (20 cm) long,
    braided
ring pull from a drinks can
2 dark-colored beads
1 dark-colored button
red felt heart, 1¼ x 1 in.
    (3 x 2 cm)

## Equipment

pencil
photograph
colored pencils
scissors
ruler
thick felt pen
dressmaking pins
needle
frame, 15¾ x 15¾ in.
    (40 x 40 cm)
staple gun
hook

*Approximate finished size:*
10 x 10 in. (25 x 25 cm)

**1** Working from the photograph, draw a design on paper and color it in. Select a range of fabrics that match the colors within the design. Prepare the fabrics by cutting them into strips approximately ½ in. (1 cm) wide and as long as possible. Using another sheet of plain paper, trace over the design, drawing the outline shapes of the main motifs.

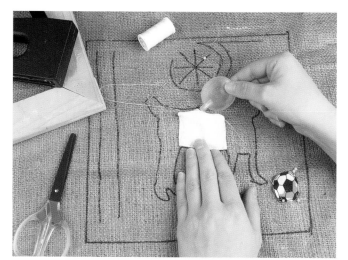

**2** Mark out a square 10 x 10 in. (25 x 25 cm) on the burlap (the same size as the design). Cut out the main motifs from the tracing. Pin the motifs in the correct places within the square and draw around them.

**3** Take the white cotton square and pin it to the center of the dog's body shape. Sew three sides of the square to the burlap with white thread using backstitch, leaving the top open to insert the squeaker (for backstitch see page 19). Place the squeaker in the "pocket" and sew up the top. Pin the football patch just below the paw on the far right of the picture. Use white double thread and sew a backstitch all around until you have a gap of approximately ¾ in. (2 cm). Take the polyester toy stuffing and push this inside to create a raised surface. Sew up the gap.

**4** Hook around the outline shape of the dog's body using white fabric strips and a loop-pile surface.

5 Continue hooking around the dog, filling in the background area in shades of green, and using both a cut- and loop-pile surface to vary the texture.

6 To make the dog's collar, take the braided length of red wool, push the hook through the burlap from the back, and hook the red wool through. Thread the ring pull onto the wool collar. Working from underneath push the hook up through the burlap and pull the end of the wool through to the back. Tie the ends of the wool together to secure them. To add the finishing touches, sew on beads to make the dog's eyes and a button for her nose. Finally, stitch the red heart into position in the bottom left hand corner. To finish off, see the method on page 24.

# wall banner
This long rectangular banner looks dramatic yet is very easy to make. Simple shapes such as hearts, hands, and flowers combined with abstract patterns make a unique work of art!

## Materials

plain paper
fabrics: wool/acrylic, jersey, cotton, nylon net, lycra
burlap, 50 x 20 in. (127 x 50 cm)
selection of buttons
selection of sequins
thread

## Equipment

pencil
colored pencils
scissors
tape measure
thick felt pen
hook
needle

*Approximate finished size:*
42 x 12 in. (107 x 30 cm)

**1** Draw a design on paper and color it in. Select a range of fabrics that match the colors within the design. Prepare the fabrics by cutting them into strips approximately ¾ in. (2 cm) wide and as long as possible.

**2** Using the tape measure and thick felt pen, draw a rectangle measuring 42 x 12 in. (107 x 30 cm) on the burlap. Approximately 6 in. (15 cm) from the bottom of the rectangle, place your hand on the burlap. With your other hand, mark a series of dots around the shape of your hand. Remove your hand and join the dots with the marker pen to show the hand shape. Mark in the other areas of the design.

**3** Begin hooking around the hand shape, working in a loop pile, alternating the shades of color.

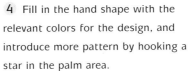

**4** Fill in the hand shape with the relevant colors for the design, and introduce more pattern by hooking a star in the palm area.

**5** Continue hooking, using a loop-pile surface throughout. Sew on buttons and sequins to add further surface texture. Enhance the pattern by hooking back through areas, making loops approximately ¾ in. (2 cm) apart to create dots of color. To finish off, follow the method on page 24.

**red banner** This is an alternative design to the pastel-colored banner. By contrasting rich reds with pale colors, a bolder effect is achieved. Appliqué is used at the ends of the banner to vary the texture.

# geometric frame
These square frames are hooked using a loop-pile surface with an equal balance of black and white. Inspired by Mexican geometric patterns, they are a stylish solution for framing small photographs.

**Materials**

plain paper
fabrics: jersey in black and
  white
burlap, 12 x 12 in.
  (30 x 30 cm)
black thread

**Equipment**

pencil
ruler
scissors
thick felt pen
embroidery hoop, 10 in.
  (25 cm) in diameter
hook

*Approximate finished size:*
6 x 6 in. (15 x 15 cm)

1  Draw out a square on paper measuring 6 x 6 in. (15 x 15 cm). Mark out a central window of 2¼ x 2¼ in. (6 x 6 cm). Using a thick felt pen, draw your design within the frame. Cut out the design. Prepare the fabrics by cutting them into strips approximately ½ in. (1 cm) wide and as long as possible.

2 Place the burlap in the embroidery hoop and pin the design to it. Draw around the edge of the design template, then carefully copy the black lines onto the burlap too.

3 Begin hooking around the inner window square in a loop pile using black fabric.

4  Continue hooking the lines in black. Change to white fabric to fill in the remainder of the design. Remove the burlap from the frame. To finish off, follow the method on page 24.

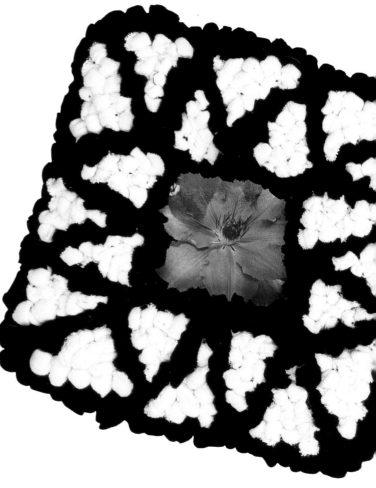

# flowery curtain

A plain net curtain has been transformed by introducing hooked tapestry wool as decoration. The flowerbed theme on this curtain uses a red and white gingham border with pom-pom seeds from which six flowers grow. Recycled shirt buttons form the centers of the flowers, surrounded by hooked long-loop petals. A crochet hook rather than a ragwork hook is used in this project as it is less likely to catch on the net of the curtain.

## Materials

plain paper
red and white gingham
   fabric, 20¾ x 4¾ in.
   (52 x 12 cm)
red tapestry wool
nylon net, 40 x 20 in.
   (100 x 50 cm)
white thread
6 white shirt buttons
3 red pom-poms
3 white pom-poms

## Equipment

pencil
colored pencils
dressmaking pins
needle
tape measure
embroidery hoop, 6 in.
   (15 cm) in diameter
crochet hook, size 3.5

*Approximate finished size:*
*40 x 20 in. (100 x 50 cm)*

**1** Sketch the design on paper and color it in. Select fabric and wool to match the colors in the design.

**2** Fold the gingham in half lengthwise and pin it along the short end of the nylon net, folding the edges under to stop them from fraying: the net should lie between the folded gingham. Use white thread to slipstitch the gingham to the net.

**3** With a tape measure, working from the bottom edge of the curtain, measure up 7½ in. (19 cm). Mark this point by sewing a white button onto the net, approximately 2 in. (5 cm) from the side.

**4** To make the red petals, place the nylon net in the embroidery hoop, take the crochet hook, and hook a loop pile approximately 1 in. (2.5 cm) high around the edge of the button.

**5** Hook a vertical stem with red wool from the flower petals down to the edge of the gingham border. Work this stem in a loop pile about ½ in. (1 cm) high. Approximately 2¼ in. (6 cm) across from the first flower make the second flower by following steps 1 to 5. Make this flower 4 in. (10 cm) tall. Continue in this way, alternating the flower heights, until you have six flowers in total.

**6** To add the finishing touch, sew alternating red and white pom-poms under each flower stem along the gingham border.

# furniture

# chair pad

Soften the seat of a wooden chair with a colorful ragwork chair pad. This project can be made for a single chair or, for the more ambitious, a matching set of chair pads could be made.

For this design a simple image of a red star framed in shades of blue has been chosen. Old T-shirts and woolens have been recycled and hooked through burlap. The blue ties prevent the chair pad from slipping off the seat.

**Materials**

fabrics: nylon, jersey,
  wool/acrylic in reds
  and blues
plain paper
brown paper
burlap, 23 x 23 in.
  (58 x 58 cm)
linen thread

**Equipment**

pencil
colored pencils
scissors
thick felt pen
frame, 15³⁄₄ x 15³⁄₄ in.
  (40 x 40 cm)
staple gun
dressmaking pins
hook

*Approximate finished size:*
12³⁄₄ x 14¹⁄₄ in. (32 x 36 cm)

1 Choose a chair. Sketch the chair pad design on paper and color it in, then select fabrics to match the design. Prepare the fabrics by cutting them into strips approximately ¹⁄₂ in. (1 cm) wide and as long as possible.

2 Using the brown paper and a thick felt pen, draw a template by laying the paper on top of the chair seat. Cut around the template. Attach the burlap to the frame using the staple gun. Pin the template to the center of the burlap and draw around it.

**3** Cut out the central star motif from the template, then pin it to the burlap in the middle of the chair seat shape. Draw around the star and unpin it.

**4** Using blue fabric, begin hooking around the outside of the chair pad shape. Hook the outline of the star motif in pink. Use a loop pile throughout.

**5** Fill in the pattern by hooking the star in shades of pink and red then working outward hook the background in shades of blue. Remove the burlap from the frame and finish it off following the method on page 22. To make the chair pad ties, cut two strips of blue jersey fabric 1 x 14 in. (2 x 35 cm). Pin them to the reverse of the chair pad in the back corners, and stitch them to the burlap with linen thread.

## multicolored throw

This throw is made from old T-shirt strips in a range of colors. A departure from working with burlap, the strips are hooked through a soft green felt backing cloth with a silky ribbon edge. The throw is reversible, one side featuring loops, the other featuring knots.

The fabric strips are hooked in shades of pumpkin orange, ruby red, pastel pink, mid blue, and purple. The colors are placed at random to create a sea of multicolored loops or knots.

**Materials**

plain paper
fabrics: a selection of cotton
   jersey (old T-shirts) in a
   minimum of 6 colors
blue ribbon, 3 yards
   (2.6 m) long
felt, 32 x 19 in.
   (81 x 48 cm)
blue thread

**Equipment**

pencil
colored pencils
dressmaking pins
needle
scissors
hook

*Approximate finished size:*
32 x 19 in. (81 x 48 cm)

**1** Sketch a design on paper and color it in. Select fabrics in assorted shades to match those of the design.

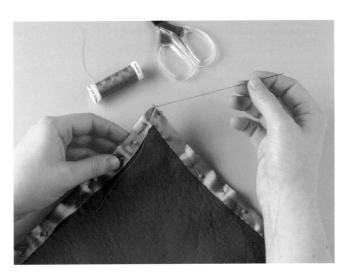

**2** Take the ribbon, fold it in half (widthwise) and pin it around the edge of the felt, so that an equal depth of ribbon is on each side. Slipstitch the ribbon to the felt. (For slipstitch see the method on page 20.)

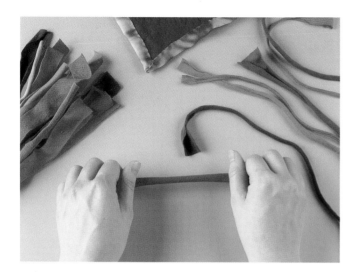

**3** Prepare the fabrics by cutting them into strips 1 in. (2 cm) wide and 8 in. (20 cm) long. Take a strip, hold it at both ends and pull. This encourages the fabric to roll around itself.

**4** Begin in one corner. Push the hook through the felt to make a hole. Approximately ½ in. (1 cm) away from the first hole, push the hook through to make a second hole.

**5** Working from underneath push the hook back through the first hole, feed the end of the first fabric strip onto the hook and pull it through the felt. Push the hook through the second hole and hook the other end of the strip through the felt.

**6** Lay the felt face down, and knot both ends of the strip.

**7** Continue hooking loops through the felt, working the colors randomly, until all of the felt is covered. Lay the throw loop-side down and trim the ends of the knots. Gently pull each loop so that both sides of the throw look tidy.

# cushion cover
Add color and texture to a plain cushion cover by attaching a hooked panel in coordinating colors. A simple felt flower shape, buttons, and mirror motifs add further detail, all framed by colorful braiding.

**Materials**

plain paper
green fabrics in cotton,
   jersey, blanket
blue pom-pom braiding,
   20 in. (50 cm) long
burlap, 9$\frac{1}{2}$ x 9$\frac{1}{2}$ in.
   (24 x 24 cm)
green felt
mirror motif
green thread
5 small pink/red buttons
pink/red thread
cushion cover, 19 x 19 in.
   (48 x 48 cm)

**Equipment**

pencil
colored pencils
embroidery hoop, 6$\frac{1}{4}$ in.
   (16 cm) in diameter
scissors
dressmaking pins
thick felt pen
hook
needle

*Approximate finished size:*
19 x 19 in. (48 x 48 cm )

1 Draw the design on paper and color it in. Select a range of fabrics and braiding to match the colors within the design.

2 Place the burlap in the embroidery hoop. Cut out the design and pin it to the burlap. Using the thick felt pen, draw around the square.

**3** Prepare the fabrics by cutting them into strips approximately ½ in. (1 cm) wide and as long as possible. Hook around the outside of the square using a loop-pile surface. Continue hooking inward until the whole square is filled.

**4** Cut out the flower shape from the paper design. Take a piece of green felt and pin the paper template to it. Cut around the flower template.

5  Pin the green felt flower to the center of the hooked square. Place the mirror motif in the center and sew it into position using a matching thread.

6  Place a pink or red button on each petal and sew them securely in place, going through the felt and the burlap, using a matching thread. Remove the burlap from the embroidery hoop. To finish off, follow the method on page 22.

7  Pin the pom-pom braiding to the back of the hooked square. Using double thread, slipstitch the braiding in place.

8  Take the cushion cover and position the hooked square in the center. With one hand inside the cushion cover, and using double thread, sew through both the hooked square and the cushion cover to secure the square in position.

# accessories

**Materials**

plain paper
fabrics: wool/acrylic, jersey,
 felt
burlap, 20 x 20 in.
 (50 x 50 cm)
star patch
purple thread
pink thread
4 pink buttons
1 ivory colored button
linen thread
2 pieces of pink felt,
 15¾ x 13¾ in.
 (40 x 34 cm) and
 8 x 4¼ in. (20 x 11 cm)
2 white pipe-cleaners 12 in.
 (30 cm) long
selection of beads,
 approximately 26 for each
 handle

**Equipment**

pencil
colored pencils
scissors
ruler
thick felt pen
dressmaking pins
needle
embroidery hoop, 12 in.
 (30 cm) in diameter
hook

*Approximate finished size:*
12½ x 6¾ in.
 (32 x 17 cm)

# bead-handled bag
Brightly colored beads and pink fringing give this bag a fun feel. The front of the bag is hooked in bold colors, with yellow wool framing shades of deep plum, fuchsia pink, and vibrant turquoise. The appliquéd felt shapes with buttons in the center add texture, and the sparkly star adds a glitzy finishing touch!

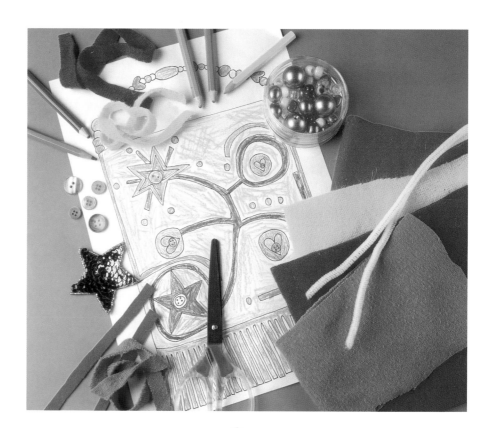

**1** Sketch the design on paper and color it in. Choose fabrics to match the colors within the design. Prepare the fabrics by cutting them into strips approximately ½ in. (1 cm) wide and as long as possible.

**2** Mark out a rectangle 12½ x 6¾ in. (32 x 17 cm) on the burlap. Cut out the main motifs from the design. Pin the motifs in the correct position within the rectangle on the burlap and draw around them. Draw the branches on the burlap.

**3** Pin the paper templates onto pieces of felt and cut around them to make circle and star shapes for appliqué. Where appropriate, cut out the inner motifs from the paper templates, pin these to felt and cut around them.

**4** Pin the felt pieces and the sparkly star into position on the burlap, and with matching thread sew around the shapes in backstitch (see the method on page 19).

**5** Sew buttons onto the center of the shapes.

6 Place the burlap in the embroidery hoop. Hook around the branch shape using purple fabric strips and a loop-pile surface.

7 Continue hooking, filling in the background in a yellow loop-pile surface. Add accents of turquoise to complete the hooking. To finish off, see the method on page 22.

8 Take a piece of felt 8 x 4¼ in. (20 x 11 cm) and, working with the shortest sides running vertically, measure 4 in. (9 cm) from the bottom up and mark this with a pin. Repeat this at short intervals along the felt until there is a horizontal line of pins. Make vertical cuts approximately ½ in. (1 cm) apart from the bottom of the felt up to the row of pins, to make a fringe.

9  Pin the fringe to the back of the hooked bag panel. Using linen thread, slipstitch along the edge of the fringe to secure it to the hooked panel (for slipstitch see page 20).

10  Take a piece of felt measuring 15¾ x 13¾ in. (40 x 34 cm), pin the top end of the felt to the back of the hooked bag panel. Slipstitch all around the felt to secure it to the panel.

11  Fold the excess felt over the back of the panel. Pin around the two sides and across the bottom. Using double pink thread, slipstitch around the three sides leaving the top open.

12  To make the handles, fold the end of a pipe-cleaner around a pencil, bend to make a loop and twist to secure. Remove the pencil to leave a hoop.

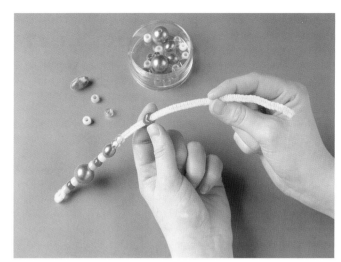

**13** Thread the beads onto the pipe-cleaner stopping 1¼ in. (3 cm) from the end. Take the pencil and bend the end of the pipe-cleaner around it to make a loop. Twist to secure.

**14** Repeat steps 12 and 13 to make a matching handle.

**15** Tuck the hoop ends of the handles inside the bag and sew through the felt and the hoops with double thread to secure them to the bag

# pom-pom purse
The colors in this design coordinate well with the bead-handled bag on page 92. The beads hold the pink ribbon in place, so you can pull it tight to keep the purse contents safe.

## Materials

plain paper
fabrics: magenta and
  turquoise woolens
selection of beads
3 small blue pom-poms
3 small purple pom-poms
burlap, 8 x 8 in.
  (20 x 20 cm)
pink felt, 8¾ x 6 in.
  (22 x 15 cm)
yellow button
pink thread
pink ribbon, 24 in. (60 cm)
  long

## Equipment

pencil
colored pencils
embroidery hoop, 7 in.
  (17 cm) in diameter
scissors
dressmaking pins
thick felt pen
hook
sewing needle
big eye tapestry needle

*Approximate finished size:*
4¼ x 4 in. (11 x 10 cm)

**1** Draw a design on paper and color it in. Select fabrics, beads, and pom-poms to match the design.

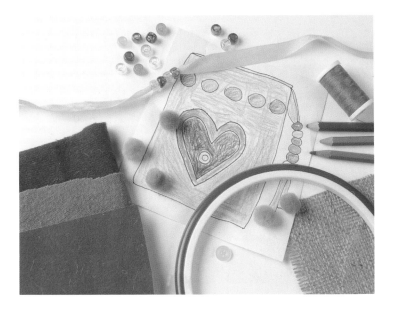

**2** Place the burlap in the embroidery hoop. Cut out the heart from the paper design and pin this in the center of the burlap. Using the thick felt pen, draw around the shape.

**3** Take the turquoise and purple woolen fabrics and cut them into strips approximately ½ in. (1 cm) wide and as long as possible. Hook around the outside of the heart in turquoise creating a loop-pile surface. Fill in the center of the heart in purple, again using a loop-pile surface.

**4** Trim across the top of the loops to create a cut-pile surface. Remove the burlap from the hoop and finish it off following the method on page 22. Now make the purse.

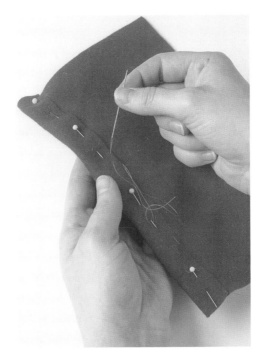

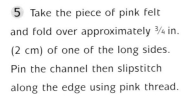

**5** Take the piece of pink felt and fold over approximately ¾ in. (2 cm) of one of the long sides. Pin the channel then slipstitch along the edge using pink thread.

**6** Fold the sewn felt in half with the stitching from step 5 on the outside and pin along the bottom and side. Using a double length of pink thread, sew a backstitch around the purse, stopping just before you reach the channel created in step 5. Turn the purse inside out.

**7** Take the hooked heart and sew a yellow button to the middle of it. Pin the heart onto the purse and, using double thread, stitch through one layer of the felt to secure it.

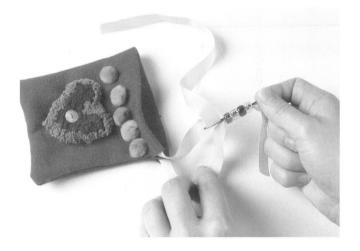

**8** Pin a row of alternating-colored pom-poms along the top of the purse just under the channel. Sew each pom-pom securely through one layer of felt.

**9** Using the big eye tapestry needle, thread the pink ribbon through the channel at the top of the purse. Thread both ends of ribbon through colored beads then tie the ends of the ribbon together to hold the beads in place.

## hair accessories

In this simple project, heart and flower shapes are hooked or appliquéd and attached to hair grips. You need never have a bad hair day again!

Recycled scraps of assorted fabrics—old saris, T-shirts, and felt off-cuts—are enhanced by adding buttons and mirror motifs. These hair accessories have been finished off in such a way that they can be slipped on and off hair grips or the hairband made on page 106.

**Materials**

plain paper
pink and green felt
mirror motif
green embroidery thread
hair grip

**Equipment**

pencil
colored pencils
scissors
dressmaking pins
needle

*Approximate finished size of the heart:*
1¼ x 1¼ in. (3 x 3 cm)

**2** Remove the template and cut off the outer border to leave a smaller heart shape. Pin this template to pink felt and cut around the edge. Lay the pink heart on top of the larger green heart. Take the mirror motif and pin it to the middle of both hearts. Using embroidery thread, sew a neat blanket stitch around the mirror motif and through both felt layers. (For blanket stitch see page 20.)

**1** Draw designs on paper, color them in, then cut them out. Pin the heart template to a small piece of green felt and cut out the shape.

3  Sew two french knots into the top left and right curves of the heart (For french knots see page 21.)

4  Cut a small rectangle of felt approximately 1 x 1¼ in. (2 x 3 cm), pin it to the back of the heart, and sew it at the top and the bottom, leaving a central channel through which a hair grip (or hairband) can be inserted.

# hairband

This hairband features four hand-hooked flowers, in shades of green, blue, red, and pink, inspired by the bold shapes and bright colors of summer blooms. The flowers are made to be slipped on to the hairband frame, so different flowers can be made to coordinate with a multitude of outfits.

## Materials

plain paper
fabrics: blue net, pink felt
burlap, 10 x 10 in.
   (25 x 25 cm)
pink buttons
thread
blue felt
metal hairband

## Equipment

pencil
colored pencils
scissors
embroidery hoop, 6¼ in.
   (16 cm) in diameter
thick felt pen
hook
needle
dressmaking pins

*Approximate finished size
of the flowers:*
3 in. (7 cm) in diameter

1  Draw a design on paper and color it in. Select a range of fabrics that match the colors within the design. Prepare the fabrics by cutting them into strips. Cut the felt ¾ in. (2 cm) wide and as long as possible. Cut the net 2 in. (4 cm) wide and as long as possible.

**2** Place the burlap in the embroidery hoop. With a thick felt pen draw a circle ³⁄₄ in. (2 cm) in diameter. Take a strip of felt and begin hooking, filling in the circle using a long loop pile.

**3** Using scissors, trim across the top of the loops to create a cut pile approximately ¹⁄₄ in. (5 mm) high.

**4** To make the petals, take a length of net and hook around the outside of the circle in a long loop pile approximately 1¼ in. (3 cm) high.

**5** Place a button in the center of the "flower," and stitch it into position using double thread. Remove the burlap from the embroidery hoop and finish it off following the method on page 22.

**6** Cut a circle of blue felt ¾ in. (2 cm) in diameter, pin it to the reverse of the flower center and slipstitch around the edge using double thread. (For slipstitch see page 20.)

**7** Cut a rectangle of felt ½ x ¾ in. (1 x 2 cm). Pin it across the back of the flower and stitch down both sides leaving a channel through the center, through which the hairband can be threaded. Make three more flowers by following steps 1 to 7.

**8** Cut one long strip of blue felt ¾ in. (2 cm) wide and as long as possible. Wind this around the metal hairband, pinning it at intervals to hold it in place.

**9** Using double thread, sew small, close stitches to attach the felt securely around the hairband.

**10** Finally, thread the flowers into position on the hairband.

# bobbly scarf

This project demonstrates how a plain scarf can be livened up by adding some multicolored woolen "bobbles" to the ends. Here, tapestry wool in five different colors was crocheted to form a loose chain and then hooked through the soft material of the scarf. This simple technique can also be used to embellish woolen skirts or sweaters.

**Materials**

plain paper
tapestry wool in pale blue,
  red, dark blue, mauve, and
  orange
woolen scarf, 27½ x 10¼ in.
  (70 x 26 cm)
thread

**Equipment**

pencil
colored pencils
crochet hook, size 3.5
scissors
tape measure
hook
needle

*Approximate finished size:*
27½ x 10¼ in. (70 x 26 cm)

**1** Sketch your design on paper and color it in. Choose five different colors of tapestry wool to match the colors within the design.

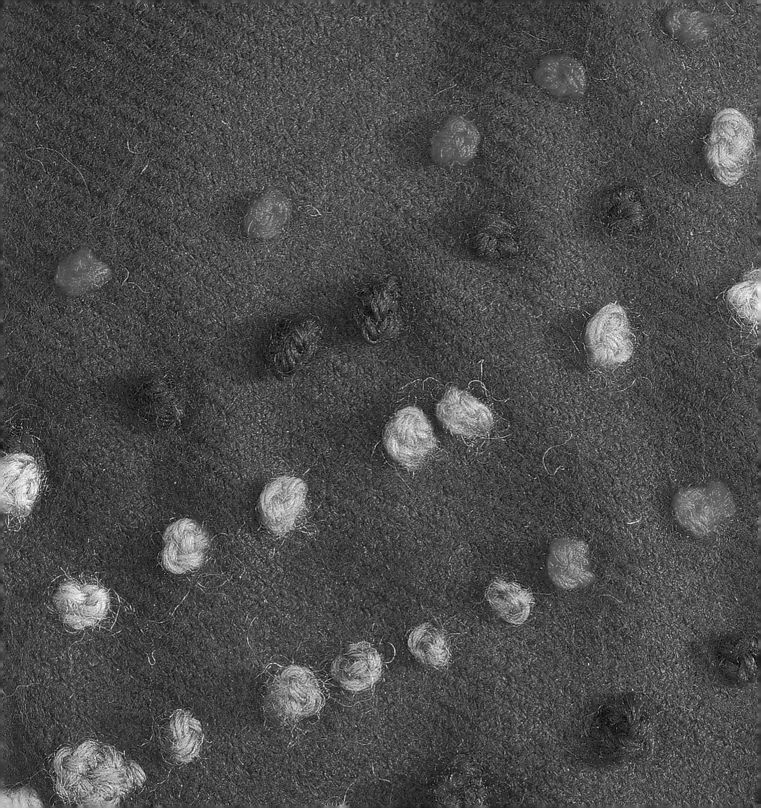

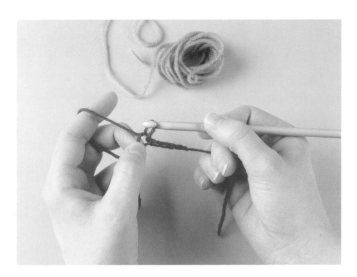

2 Make a slip loop with the first color of tapestry wool and thread this onto the crochet hook. Twist the hook first under then over the yarn to wind the wool around the hook. Draw the hook through the slip loop to begin the chain. Repeat this action until the chain is approximately 6 in. (15 cm) long (see page 21).

3 Finish the chain by cutting the wool, placing the end through the final loop of the chain and tying a knot. Continue crocheting chains of approximately the same length, alternating the colors. This project uses 14 crocheted chains.

4 Lay the scarf on a flat surface and measure 6 in. (15 cm) up from the scarf fringe. Begin hooking the first crocheted chain through the woolen scarf at intervals of approximately 1 in. (2 cm). The crocheted strips can be secured by stitching them to the back of the scarf.

# patches Colorful patches can be used to brighten up all sorts of things, from denim jackets to cushions. Simple shapes work best: hearts, fish, flowers, and birds can all be hooked on a small scale.

In this project, a heart patch is hooked in red and three pink roses are added. The patch can be either sewn directly to a jacket or pinned on as a brooch.

**Materials**

plain paper
red stretchy fabric
burlap, 9 x 9 in.
  (23 x 23 cm)
3 fabric roses on wire

**Equipment**

pencil
colored pencils
scissors
embroidery hoop, 6¼ in.
  (16 cm) in diameter
dressmaking pins
thick felt pen
hook

*Approximate finished size:*
3 x 3½ in. (8 x 9 cm)

**1** Sketch design on paper and color it in. Cut the fabric into strips approximately ½ in. (1 cm) wide and as long as possible.

2  Place the burlap in the embroidery hoop, cut out the heart template and pin it to the center of the burlap. Using the thick felt pen draw around the template.

3  Unpin the template and begin hooking around the outside of the heart shape using a loop pile.

4 Continue hooking, filling in the shape. Take the three roses and position them on the heart, then push the wire stems through the burlap.

5 Turn the frame face down on a flat surface and bend back the wire stems of the three roses to secure them in position. To finish off, follow the method on page 22.

# decorated slippers These fun slippers will keep your feet warm in style! By using character or shaped buttons in the center of each motif, fine detail is easily achieved. The motifs are attached to the slippers with Velcro, so can be interchanged to suit your mood.

## SCOTTIE MOTIFS

### Materials

plain paper

tartan ribbon, ¾ x 4¾ in.
  (2 x 12 cm)

green felt

2 scottie dog buttons

burlap, 11 x 11 in.
  (28 x 28 cm)

red thread

red Velcro strip, 2 x ¾ in.
  (4 x 2 cm)

slippers

### Equipment

colored pencils

embroidery hoop, 6¾ in.
  (17 cm) in diameter

scissors

dressmaking pins

needle

hook

*Approximate finished size
of scottie motifs:*

2 in. (5 cm) in diameter

1 Draw designs based on your buttons.
We have used hearts and scottie dogs.
Color them in. Choose ribbon and felt to
match the scottie design.

**2** Place the burlap in the embroidery hoop. Cut a piece of ribbon approximately 1³/₄ in. (4 cm) long. Fold the ends of the ribbon under to prevent them from fraying. Pin the ribbon to the center of the burlap.

**3** Using red thread, stitch the ribbon to the burlap. Take a scottie dog button and sew this to the center of the ribbon.

**4** Take the green felt and cut it into strips approximately ¹/₄ in. (5 mm) wide and as long as possible. Hook a long loop pile approximately ³/₄ in. (2 cm) high all around the ribbon square. Remove the burlap from the embroidery hoop. To finish off, follow the method on page 22.

**5** Take the Velcro strip and cut it in half. Pin the female/non-abrasive side to the back of the hooked square, and slipstitch around it using double thread.

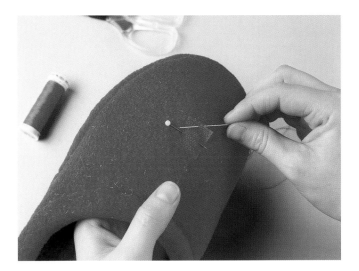

**6** Take the male/abrasive side of the Velcro, pin it to the slipper, and slipstitch around it using double thread. Repeat steps 2 to 6 to make a matching motif for the other slipper.

# DAISY MOTIFS

## Materials

plain paper
burlap, 11 x 11 in.
   (28 x 28 cm)
tartan ribbon, ¾ x 40 in.
   (2 x 100 cm)
2 green felt circles, ¾ in.
   (2 cm) in diameter
2 red heart buttons
red thread
red Velcro strip, 1¾ x ¾ in.
   (4 x 2 cm)
slippers

## Equipment

pencil
colored pencils
embroidery hoop, 7 in.
   (17 cm) in diameter
scissors
hook
dressmaking pins
needle

*Approximate finished size
of daisy motifs:*

3½ in. (8 cm) in diameter

**1** Select fabrics to match the colors in the daisy design. Place the burlap in the embroidery hoop. Cut the tartan ribbon in half, to make two strips ¾ x 20 in. (2 x 50 cm) long. Working in the center of the burlap, hook a circle of six petals in long loops, approximately 1¾ in. (4 cm) high.

**2** Take a circle of green felt and position this in the center of the petals. Place a red heart button on top of the felt and stitch the button through the green felt and the burlap. Remove the burlap from the hoop. To finish off, follow the method on page 22.

To complete this project follow steps 5 and 6 of the scottie motifs on page 123.

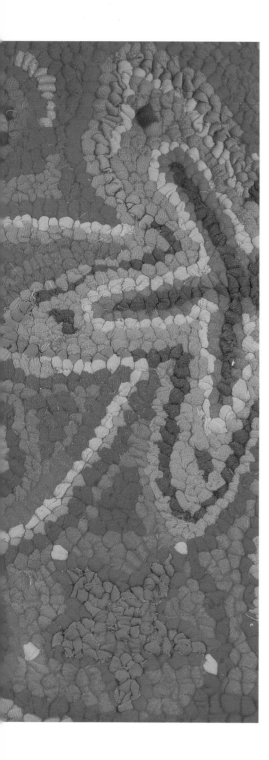

# Index

# Acknowledgments

A big thank you to all at Breslich & Foss—to Janet Ravenscroft for her initial enthusiasm and inspiration, to Katy Lord for her guidance, good humor and bread-and-butter pudding, and to Janet James for great design and layout. Special thanks to Shona Wood for her beautiful photography. Love to Anne and Keith for their time and patience with Pickles, and love to J and P for the loan of Spot.

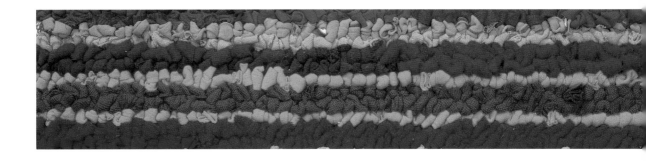